"THE WORLD'S EASIEST POCKET GUIDE"

— TO —

Creating Your First

Financial
Plan

"THE WORLD'S EASIEST POCKET GUIDE"

— TO —

Creating Your First Financial Plan

LARRY BURKETT

WITH ED STRAUSS
ILLUSTRATED BY KEN SAVE

MOODY PRESS
CHICAGO

For Lightwave Publishing
Managing Editor: *Rick Osborne*
Project Assistant: *Mikal Marrs*
Text Director: *Christie Bowler*
Art Director: *Terry van Roon*
Research: *Todd Martin*

Text & Illustrations © 2001 BURKETT & KIDS, LLC
Executive Producer: *Allen Burkett*

ISBN: 0-8024-0994-6

1 3 5 7 9 10 8 6 4 2

Printed in the United States of America

Table of Contents

How to Use This Book 6

Chapter 1
Knowing Where You're Going 7

Chapter 2
I Have a Dream 13

Chapter 3
A Polaroid of Your Pocketbook 19

Chapter 4
Developing a Budget 25

Chapter 5
The Long and the Short of It 31

Chapter 6
Getting Organized 39

Chapter 7
Reining in Wild Horses 43

Chapter 8
Dealing with Debt 49

Chapter 9
Increasing Your Earnings 53

Chapter 10
Implementing Your Plan 59

Glossary 62

Index 63

How to Use This Book

Shortly after leaving home, many young adults embark on a learning curve so drastic that it resembles a roller-coaster ride. Things they never did before—such as holding down a full-time job, paying bills, saving money, renting an apartment, using a credit card—suddenly become sink-or-swim survival skills. Most people fail to learn these basics while still at home and are woefully unprepared for life in the real world when they move out on their own.

The first four books in this series—*Getting Your First Credit Card, Buying Your First Car, Renting Your First Apartment,* and *Preparing for College*—were written to teach you the basic life skills you need to survive in today's jungle. In these four new books, *Your First Full-Time Job, Your First Savings Plan, Your First Investment,* and *Your First Financial Plan,* we walk you step-by-step through getting and keeping a job, saving money, investing money without losing your shirt, and getting and keeping control of your money.

These books contain a wealth of commonsense tips. They also give sound advice from a godly, biblical perspective. It is our prayer that the books in this series will save you from having to learn these things in the "school of hard knocks."

To get the most out of these books, you should photocopy and complete the checklists and forms we've included. We provided them to help you take on these new tasks step-by-step and to make these books as practical as possible.

Each book contains a glossary to explain commonly used terms. If at any point while reading you need a clear definition of a certain word or term, you can look it up. Each book also contains a helpful index that allows you to find pages where a key word or subject is mentioned in the book.

CHAPTER 1

Knowing Where You're Going

Knowing Where You're Going

The Man with No Plan

Nabal inherited one hundred gold bars when his father died. Now it has to be said that Nabal didn't have good money management skills, but he did have a vision. And *what* a vision! He decided to become one of the wealthiest, most influential merchants in Babylon by building a massive tower near the city docks and storing goods for a price.

Nabal shelled out gold to buy the land and, of course, bribed quite a number of officials to get them to approve the deal. Several greasy palms later, he hired an architect to draw up plans. Nabal had no idea how much it would cost to build the tower, but he figured he had more than enough. He told the builder to buy all the stones and timbers he needed and hire the workers. Done. They went to work and after a month the foundation was laid.

And that was *it*. Nabal was broke. He had nothing left to build the tower itself. He asked his in-laws to lend him money, but the answer was no. He begged the moneylenders, but they laughed. Worse yet, no one wanted to buy his plot of ground. It sat there filling up with water, becoming a breeding ground for frogs.

Nabal had a vision. He had money to help make that dream come true. Why did he fail? He didn't have a financial plan. Crazy? You say no one would act so foolishly? Oh, you would be surprised. Millions of Americans drift through life squandering their potential with the same lack of planning. They have dreams but they fail because they don't sit down, look at the price tag, and check that against their wallets.

Jesus said, "Suppose one of you wants to build a tower. Will he not first sit down and estimate the cost to see if he has enough money to complete it? For if he lays the foundation and is not able to finish it, everyone who sees it will ridicule him, saying, 'This fellow began to build and was not able to finish'" (Luke 14:28–30).

Jesus was talking about counting the cost of becoming His disciple. He wanted you to know that you need to make a wholehearted, thought-out commitment so that later on you won't quit halfway through your Christian walk. But the principles He laid out in this parable also apply to the financial areas of your life. You not only need a clear commitment to live for Jesus, you also need a life plan—and a financial plan to put wheels on that life plan.

Life Plan and Financial Plan

You simply *must* have a vision and a direction for your life. A life plan helps you with that. It is based upon a knowledge of your talents and gifts and includes what you believe the specific will of God is for your life. It also includes some intermediary steps along the way to what God wants you to do. A big part of making that vision a reality is a financial plan. A vision without a specific plan to make it happen is merely a daydream.

Your financial plan takes your life plan with its intermediate and long-term goals, puts a price tag on those things, and shows you how to get the needed money. Your financial plan lets you see just how much cash it's going to take to reach your goals and accomplish your vision. It will tell you exactly how long—saving at your present rate—you will take to get there. It also makes sure you don't need to scramble to pay your bills every month. It makes sure that your bills get paid in full and on time, and that there's food on the table—and a dream in the making.

Why You Need Plans

Often Christians question whether they should do *any* planning. Their question is: "Shouldn't a Christian depend totally on God?" Yes. But letting God lead doesn't mean letting God do all the work of bringing about His plan.

If you have a life plan, you'll be focused and single-minded. Without one you'll wander aimlessly from job to job, goal to goal (if you even have a goal). You won't be focused. Your time and energy will be squandered on half a dozen half-finished dreams. Having a life plan is vital.

But a life plan alone is not enough. Your heart may ache for the poor in Africa and you may have a vision to donate years of your life as a medical missionary. But if you do not have a plan of exactly what it will take to get there—what training and experience you'll need, how much that education will cost, and how you are going to get the money for it—chances are that you won't fulfill your vision.

You absolutely *must* have a life plan to give you purpose and direction. And you absolutely *must* have a detailed financial plan to give you the nuts and bolts of how much moola this dream is going to cost. You *must* also have a time schedule and checkpoints along the way to measure actual progress against predicted progress—reality checks to verify whether you are still on track and on schedule.

Planning versus Default Thinking

If you believe that God wants you to be a teacher who coaches disadvantaged kids on the side and who has lots of time to be involved at church—congratulations! You have a life plan.

But if you have no financial plan, when it comes time to figure out how you're going to pay for the education your dream requires, your brain will probably flip into default thinking: You'll finance your education, the way most young people finance their educations—by taking out a student loan.

This may seem like the easy route, but if you take out a loan to finance your education, you could end up forced to take a "meantime job" afterwards to pay bills and repay the loan. Years may go by with you never landing the job you wanted or fulfilling your dreams. Many idealistic young people who set out with stars in their eyes have found themselves so laden with debt after college that they were unable to do much more than pay their bills. Their lack of a financial plan meant their life plan was off the rails and never got back on.

Think about Nabal who had to abandon building his tower. Is there really any difference between a man committing every bit of his finances to building a tower without calculating the price tag and a young person committing herself to paying back a $40,000 student loan without realizing that it will take years of her life to pay it back with its high interest?

If you have a financial plan in place, you can avoid falling into default thinking. Default thinking these days is typically debt mentality. This has resulted in millions of partially built towers strewn across America as monuments to financial shortsightedness. Millions of people begin a financial journey without planning properly and without "estimating the cost," and end up in serious debt or even bankruptcy . . . with their dreams in rubble at their feet.

This usually leads to another kind of default thinking: People who are unable to reach their life's goals often simply give up on their dreams and opt for a second-best goal.

When you begin with a plan, you will realize early on that your life's goal costs more than you have. The result? You'll get the finances in place before you begin to build your "tower," or you'll at least have plans for how to get the money at each stage along the way.

What? Me, Worry?

Another benefit of having a financial plan is that it takes so much uncertainty and stress out of your day-to-day routine. You might say, "What? Me, worry? I'm not concerned about my finances or my future!" Really? There are very few people who *aren't* bothered by these things. A recent study showed that 75 percent of college freshmen are concerned about their financial security. This is a huge increase from the 1970 data that reported that only 44 percent had this concern. Whether you are concerned about your financial future or not, you will still need to deal with it.

What a Plan Will Do for You

A financial plan will do the following things for you:

(1) It will help you achieve your dreams.

(2) It will give you more control over your future. Once you prioritize your goals and decide what is important in your life, you put money in savings to invest in that future and make it a reality.

(3) It will stop you from spending more than you have coming in. This will keep you from racking up debt and wasting money on interest payments.

(4) It will stop impulse buying. Rather than being wasted on junk you don't need, your hard-earned cash will go where you planned for it to go and pay bills you *must* pay.

(5) It will remove confusion and uncertainty and keep you from being surprised by forgotten bills. You'll know exactly what bills to pay when you get your paycheck.

(6) It will allow you to set aside money for unexpected financial emergencies not covered by insurance.

(7) It will give you a good credit rating. As we show later, this is a big bonus!

Now it's time to move on to the next chapter and begin deciding what your life plan is and what God has called you to be.

CHAPTER 2

I Have a Dream

"Lord, we give You our goals, dreams, and plans. We commit these to You and ask that *Your will* would be done for each of us..."

1 Have a Dream

Desires, Goals, and Dreams

Psalm 37:4 says, "Delight yourself in the LORD and he will give you the desires of your heart." These "desires" can range from a milk shake on a hot day to a career studying algae growth rates in Queen Maud Land, Antarctica. Mind you, we usually call a milk shake a "desire," and a career a "goal."

A dream on the other hand might be pure pleasure—like visiting all fifty states of the Union—or it may be giving your time to some worthwhile cause unrelated to your work. It could be learning New Testament Greek, going on a missions trip to Lapland, or owning a hobby farm raising ostriches. When you're a young adult, most of your goals and dreams will have to do with the education you need, the career you want to work in, and world-changing causes you want to be part of.

What are the desires of *your* heart? What is your dream and what is your "dream job"? A good way to figure out what you really want is to lay on top of a haystack at night and look up at the sky full of stars and imagine what you'd be doing if you were in the career you loved and were born to do. Your dream job may be a good indication of where God wants you to be. (If you don't have a haystack, a bed will do.) Dream about what you would do if money was no issue at all. Dare to dream of things that you think may be impossible.

Count God In

Solomon advised in Proverbs 16:3, "Commit to the LORD whatever you do, and your plans will succeed." Whatever financial plan you now have, set it out in the sun before God and let Him have a good look at it. "In his heart a man plans his course, but the LORD determines his steps" (Proverbs 16:9). Bring God into your planning processes early. He's going to have His way eventually, so why waste time on plans He might

14

have to change later?

Part of laying your plan out in plain sight includes sharing it with people—family and friends—whose opinions you respect. They may see problems in areas where you have a blind spot, especially if they're older and have experienced the pitfalls and challenges you're facing. This includes career counselors who can help you with personality and aptitude tests. So tell them what you have come up with and ask for their input.

Online Personality Test

There's also help on the Internet. Take a look at a personality test online. If you have access to a computer, go to *www.cfcministry.org* and select *Life Pathways* on the left-hand column. Click on *Personality I.D.™* and do the survey. The result could be an eye-opener—or give a clearer focus on things you already knew.

God made you and knows all about you. He designed you for a specific purpose, one that suits you to a T. So finding out what you're good at and love to do can help you figure out God's place for you. But bear in mind that God wants you to grow and learn as well. Sure, you may be shy and may not feel you could be an auctioneer, but Moses thought he couldn't speak in public either. God said He would help Moses and teach him (Exodus 4:10–12).

Saving Your Life

If you're a Christian and have dedicated your life to Jesus, you already have the most important chunk of your life plan in place. You have given up your own self-centered goals, desires, and plans. You have determined to live your life loving God and others, and obeying the principles in His Word.

Jesus said, "Whoever wants to save his life will lose it, but whoever loses his life for me will find it" (Matthew 16:25). Want to really find life? Want the best life plan of all? Give up your own self-centered life goals and let God guide your planning. This doesn't mean that if you love the great outdoors, fishing, and hiking, you'll never be able to do those things again. God wants to give you the desires of your heart. They'll just be lower on the list.

Writing out a life plan is not something you do in one day. A life plan is something you should have already given a great deal of prayer and thought to. But let's see where you're at to date—assuming that you've done your dreaming on the haystack and have the results of your personality test.

Writing a Mission Statement

Start off by writing out a mission statement. Write in two brief sentences what you believe is the purpose for your life. Name the goal you believe you should aim your time, energy, and money toward. Putting even a brief vision on paper will do wonders to help you focus your thoughts and ensure that what you do is driven by a purpose.

Try to be specific and honest. For example, a life goal might be: "To do pharmaceutical research in the rain forests of Brazil, discovering new miracle drugs. To speak fluent Portuguese so I can preach the gospel to the river villages and teach the Bible to strengthen believers." Or your goal might be: "To be a police officer, specializing in community relations, to build bridges to the public. To be active in my church and to support inner-city outreaches to gangs."

By writing down your vision, you dramatically increase your odds of achieving that vision because now you have something that you can look at every day to remind you what your focus is. By writing it out, you are laying out the course for the race you'll run. "Write the vision and make it plain on tablets, that he may run who reads it" (Habakkuk 2:2 NKJV).

Writing Out Goals

The form *Life/Financial Plan* on page 18 is the heart of this book. By the time you've completed all the chapters and filled out this form—and you'll do this step-by-step as you go through the book—you'll have your financial plan in place.

Make a few copies of this form, enlarging it so you have enough space to write. When you've worked over your mission statement and are happy with it, write it at the top in the

Mission Statement (Career) space. After you have done this, write your Personal Goals in the Goals & Dreams column. These Personal Goals may dovetail closely with your career— e.g., preaching in river villages or hunting piranhas while doing pharmaceutical research in the Amazon basin. Or they may have nothing to do with your career: Perhaps you'll become a bricklayer with a passion for mountain biking and hang gliding.

Whatever the case, most dreams worth dreaming have price tags—hence the three columns on the right of the *Life/Financial Plan*. In chapter 5 we'll show you how to fill them in. For now, leave them blank. Once you've completed this form, you will have a goal, know how much it costs, and have an idea when you'll have saved up enough to make the dream come to pass.

Intermediate Plans

Your Mission Statement describes your goals, your career, your personal dreams, and where you want to be. Now how do you get there? Obviously, you can't do it in one big leap—you need to take many intermediate steps. These may include earning money to pay for your college education, getting that education, getting relevant work experience, and saving for your marriage, a house, retirement, etc.

(Preparing for your "dream job" is covered in detail in the book *Your First Full-Time Job,* and saving up for long-term life goals is covered extensively in *Your First Savings Plan.* We recommend that you buy those two books. In the meantime, however, let's work with what we have.)

You'll need to know where you're beginning from before you can make realistic plans. We'll cover the section *Where I'm at Now* in chapter 3. For now leave it blank.

Beneath your Mission Statement, write three or four intermediate steps that you will need to take to get there. For example, if you have the Amazon vision, your steps would very likely be to (1) study Portuguese, (2) go on a short-term missions trip to Brazil, (3) study pharmaceutics in college, (4) go to Bible school.

(We'll deal more fully with short-term and long-term goals—including retirement goals—in chapter 5.)

Life/Financial Plan

Mission Statement (Career):

_____

_____

_____

Goals & Dreams	Total Cost	Saved Monthly	Date Will Achieve
Intermediate Goals (Steps):			
1. _____	_____	_____	_____
2. _____	_____	_____	_____
3. _____	_____	_____	_____
4. _____	_____	_____	_____
Personal Goals:			
General:			
1. _____	_____	_____	_____
2. _____	_____	_____	_____
Short-term:			
1. _____	_____	_____	_____
2. _____	_____	_____	_____
Long-term:			
1. Auto	_____	_____	_____
2. College	_____	_____	_____
3. Marriage	_____	_____	_____
4. House	_____	_____	_____
5. Other	_____	_____	_____
6. Other	_____	_____	_____
Retirement Goals:			
1. _____	_____	_____	_____
2. _____	_____	_____	_____
Where I'm at Now:	_____	_____	_____

CHAPTER 3

A Polaroid of Your Pocketbook

"We just determined our *net* worth. And as you can see...it's better than we expected!"

A Polaroid of
Your Pocketbook

Where You're At

So now you know where you're going. Before you can clearly
see how to get there from here, you need to know where "here"
is. To develop your life plan and your financial plan you need
to take inventory of where you're at right now. You have a mission statement—where you *want* to be—so if you can accurately
state where you *are,* you'll know how much distance you have
to cover to get from here to there.

In order to get a good handle on your present financial
position, you must consider several factors: your current
monthly earnings, your regular bills, your total debts, money
you have in savings accounts, etc. Of course, getting a feel for
your financial health means more than just cracking open the
piggy bank and counting and rolling the pennies. It means ana-
lyzing your whole approach to finances as well.

Your Financial Personality

Before you look at the raw numbers and harsh reality of your
finances, take inventory of what you're doing well—and what
you're not doing so well—with your finances. Take time to
think about how you view money and to understand your
financial personality. You didn't know you had a "financial personality," whatever that is? Then step right up! Ask yourself the
following questions and ponder your answers.

- Did your family openly discuss issues or decisions that
  affected everyone?

- Do you come from a background where money was never or
  always discussed?

- What are your childhood recollections about money? How

do you feel about these memories?

- Did your parents have a budget or was it "feast and famine" every month? How did that make you feel?
- Did you receive an allowance? What do you feel about that?
- Did your parents pay you to do chores? Why or why not?
- Did you have an after school job? What did it teach you?
- What are your best and worst financial habits?
- Are you tight—even stingy—with your money? Why?
- Do you give money and gifts away freely? Why?
- Do you run up debts by being too generous with others? How do you feel about that?
- Do you buy things on impulse? Do you know why?
- Do you have a written budget that you stick to?
- Do you have money in a savings account? How much? How do you feel about that?
- Do you spend every penny you earn before the month is out? If so, do you know why you do?

These are not easy questions to answer, but answering them can help you realize what views you hold about money, whether they're conscious or not. To a degree, your background will shape your current outlook on finances and financial planning. You might need to change those views.

Checking the Checklist

Use the following checklist to evaluate your approach to financial planning. There is no score on this assessment, just an opportunity to look at how much planning you are actually doing and how you are currently handling your finances. Pat yourself on the back for areas where you're doing well and look for ways to improve in the other areas.

You might want to use a pencil to check the columns. That way, in a week or two, when you've had time to put these principles into practice, you can do this same checklist, erase your first responses, and write in your new ones.

A Financial Planning Checklist

	Got It Mastered	Could Use Improvement	Oops!
I have a clear idea of God's purpose for my finances.	_____	_____	_____
My commitment to financially support the church is solid.	_____	_____	_____
I have written down my long- and short-term goals.	_____	_____	_____
I set aside money to achieve specific goals.	_____	_____	_____
I have built up three months' worth of emergency money.	_____	_____	_____
I know how my parents influenced my views on finances.	_____	_____	_____
I have a budget and track my monthly income and expenses.	_____	_____	_____
I have a filing system to keep track of my financial records.	_____	_____	_____
I have determined to get out of debt on a set period of time.	_____	_____	_____
I avoid impulse buying and plan all my purchases.	_____	_____	_____
I pay off the entire balance on my credit card when it's due.	_____	_____	_____
I am putting money toward a retirement plan.	_____	_____	_____
I save for major purchases to avoid high credit charges.	_____	_____	_____
I regularly monitor my financial plan and make changes.	_____	_____	_____
I often try to improve myself and my earning potential.	_____	_____	_____

Your Net Worth

Your net worth is like a photograph of where you stand financially at a given moment in time. You determine your net worth by listing your money and possessions (assets), then listing your debts (liabilities). Make a photocopy of the form below, add up both categories, then subtract total liabilities from total assets. The result is your Net Worth. If your liabilities are more than your assets, you have a *negative* net worth. In other words, you're in debt.

Note: If you have more than one savings account, write the total of all your accounts in the Amount space. For Personal things, add up the total cash value of all your possessions. Write in the current market value—not what you paid for these things but what you'd get if you tried to sell them today.

ASSETS		LIABILITIES	
Money & Assets	*Amount:*	*Money Owed To:*	*Amount:*
Bank (checking)	$_____	Parents	$_____
Bank (savings)	$_____	Friends	$_____
Stocks/Bonds	$_____	Student loan	$_____
Mutual funds	$_____	Credit card(s)	$_____
Insurance (value)	$_____	Dept. store cards	$_____
$ Owed to you	$_____	Bank (for auto)	$_____
House	$_____	Installment plans	$_____
Vehicle(s)	$_____	Mortgage	$_____
Personal things	$_____	Other	$_____
Other	$_____	Other	$_____
Total: $_____		**Total:** $_____	

Total Assets	$_____
Total Liabilities	$_____
Net Worth	$_____

You should now have a clear idea of where you're at financially, so this would be the perfect time to go back to your *Life/Financial Plan* and fill in Where I'm at Now. Write a brief summary of your financial status.

Tracking Expenses

It's time to take a couple more snapshots. To do this, you will have to get a sheet of paper and create your own form. Write the month at the top, then under a heading Income, list all the money you received last month: wages, gifts, allowances, interest on savings, dividends, etc., and total the amounts.

Now, on the same sheet of paper, write down all your expenses for that month. Set it up to look like this:

EXPENSES

Date:	Item:	Amount:	Budgeted? Yes No
_____	_____	$_____	____ ____
_____	_____	$_____	____ ____
_____	_____	$_____	____ ____

Use categories from the Liabilities column on the previous chart on page 23, since you pay many of those bills monthly. Add things like rent, electricity, gas, telephone, groceries, clothing, entertainment, etc. Guess the purchases you don't have receipts for. If you bought something on the installment plan, write in the payment you made last month. In the last column—Budgeted?—check whether you planned to make that purchase or bought it on impulse.

Now compare the income for the month to the expenditures. What kind of shape are you in? By now you may be realizing that your spending habits are out of control, like a team of stampeding horses taking your stagecoach toward the cliffs. It's time to grab the reins and bring your financial horsepower under control. Once you've done this, you can start guiding those horses along the right trail—leading to financial freedom.

CHAPTER 4

Developing a Budget

"You really look glum."

"Yeah, we finally did our budget. Looks like it's *goodbye* to expensive restaurants three times a week, movies twice a week, monthly visits to the resort..."

Developing a Budget

Do You Have a Budget?

It's Friday and you've just received your first paycheck from the Pink Flamingo Co. You'd like to believe you took the job because you love people to find pink flamingos stuck in their front lawn next to that "Happy Birthday" sign. The reality is that you needed the money—and now you have it.

What are you going to do with it? If you don't know exactly how many dollars you're going to allot to every monthly expense, you don't have a budget. If all you know is that the rent needs to be paid, but you figure that the rest of your money goes to bills or items in the store window on a "first come, first spend" basis, you're in trouble. *Big* trouble . . . as you may have discovered in the previous chapter.

A monthly budget is essential if you hope to bring your day-to-day spending under control and start moving toward your goals. It is the basic building block of a financial plan, a list of what you plan to do with your money before you get it.

If you think a budget is a financial straitjacket, a killjoy designed to drain all the fun out of life, think again. It's a step toward freedom. Besides, like it or not, your money has certain obligations to meet—like food and rent. We highly recommend the budget on page 27—*Monthly Income & Expenses*. In most major categories, this budget reflects national consumer spending patterns. In other words, Americans have to spend their money this way anyway; everyone needs the same basics. And you might as well *plan* to spend the money that you will *have* to spend.

Fine-tuning a budget will take some practice, so make photocopies of the *Monthly Income & Expenses* page, then take a copy and fill it in as you proceed. Before anything else, fill in both your Annual Income and Monthly Income, your gross (before taxes) income, at the top of the chart. Now let's take a look at where all that money goes.

Monthly Income & Expenses

Annual Income _____
Monthly Income _____

LESS
1. Charitable Giving _____
2. Tax _____

NET SPENDABLE INCOME _____

3. Housing (30%) _____
  Mortgage (Rent) _____
  Insurance _____
  Taxes _____
  Electricity _____
  Gas _____
  Water _____
  Sanitation _____
  Telephone _____
  Maintenance _____
  Other _____

4. Food (17%) _____

5. Auto(s) (15%) _____
  Payments _____
  Gas & Oil _____
  Insurance _____
  License _____
  Taxes _____
  Maint/Repair/
    Replacement _____

6. Insurance (5%) _____
  Life _____
  Medical _____
  Other _____

7. Debts (5%) _____
  Credit Cards _____
  Loans & Notes _____
  Other _____

8. Enter./Recreation (7%) _____
  Eating Out _____
  Trips _____
  Baby-Sitters _____
  Activities _____
  Vacation _____
  Other _____

9. Clothing (5%) _____

10. Savings (5%) _____

11. Medical Expenses (5%) _____
  Doctor _____
  Dental _____
  Drugs _____
  Other _____

12. Miscellaneous (6%) _____
  Toiletry, Cosmetics _____
  Beauty, Barber _____
  Laundry, Cleaning _____
  Allowances, Lunches _____
  Subscriptions, Gifts _____
    (Incl. Christmas)
  Special Education _____
  Cash _____
  Other _____

TOTAL EXPENSES _____

Net Spendable Income _____

Difference _____

Charitable Giving

The first category on the budget is Charitable Giving. This means giving back to God, the source of all supply. The Bible advises you, "Remember the LORD your God, for it is he who gives you the ability to produce wealth" (Deuteronomy 8:18). So what's a good way to "remember" God and keep it crisp and clear in your mind that everything you have comes from Him? Proverbs 3:9 says, "Honor the LORD with your wealth, with the firstfruits of all your crops."

In the Old Testament, God established the tithe: His people were to give one tenth of all their earnings to Him (Leviticus 27:30). They were to do this first, before paying any of their bills and hand their tithes to the priests and Levites who worked in the temple. It was God's cash, but He wanted it to be given to the Levites (Numbers 18:21, 24).

Translating this principle into today's setting, many Christians give one tenth of their earnings to their church and to missionaries. You may argue that tithing is a part of the Mosaic Law, no longer applicable in this age of grace, but the point remains, you *are* to "honor the LORD with your wealth," to demonstrate that you are thankful for His provision and to acknowledge that you are dependent on His provision. And you are to do this *first,* before paying any other bills.

So calculate 10 percent of your gross monthly income and write that figure in the Charitable Giving blank. If you feel that God wants you to give some other percentage, write *that* figure in. If you determine to give $100/month, write that in.

You may ask, "Do I *have* to give a set percentage or amount every month?" Yes. For *your* sake. Make God a priority and you'll be amazed how far the rest goes. Doing this gets you in the regular habit of giving, something you might tend to neglect when you have lots of bills. More importantly, giving to God keeps you aware that everything belongs to God and that *He* is responsible for looking after you.

Decide exactly how much you will give and stick to it. "Each man should give what he has decided in his heart to give" (2 Corinthians 9:7).

Taxes and NSI

In many cases, your boss will have deducted your taxes before he or she handed you your paycheck. You earned gross income, but after giving to God and allowing the IRS to take their share, what is left is your Net Spendable Income (NSI). If your taxes were not automatically deducted, put money aside for this expense. Stash it in a savings account and don't touch it. You do *not* want an unexpected visit from the Internal Revenue Service.

Now calculate how much your NSI is and write that figure in the blank beside Net Spendable Income. Your NSI is what you have available to pay bills and build your dreams with.

Expenses—Ideal versus Realistic

Before filling out a realistic budget, fill out a copy of the budget "by the book," according to the percentages given. Start with Housing: Calculate 30 percent of your NSI and write that dollar amount in the blank to the right of Housing. If your NSI is $1,000/month, write $300 in Housing. (The total expenses in all categories should add up to exactly 100 percent of your NSI.)

After you've assigned "ideal" dollar amounts to each category from Housing to Miscellaneous, divide the money for each category into its subcategories.

When you've filled out the ideal budget form, fill out a second photocopy using your actual expenses. You'll find in some categories that your bills are less or more than the recommended percentages. If you're living at home and housing costs nothing, great! This is not considered a problem—it's nothing to go into trauma about. It means you have more money to put in Savings toward your college education or some other goal.

What if your bills are higher than these percentages? These numbers aren't carved in stone, but they do work and they do reflect reality. (For example, this budget allows 30 percent for Housing. The average national expense is 32.7 percent.) If your housing costs 43 percent of your income, we suggest you move to cheaper lodgings. Otherwise you'll need to make serious cuts in other categories to be able to pay rent.

Now begins the laborious—but rewarding—task of bringing your budget into line. Adjust the amounts in each category until the totals line up with reality and add up to 100 percent of your NSI—not a penny more. It can be painful to realize that you can no longer spend 20 percent of your cash on Entertainment/Recreation. You'll have to cut back and make some serious lifestyle changes or find a cheaper way to entertain yourself. But exercising self-control in spending is very rewarding when it liberates money desperately needed for other categories.

Your Credit Rating

One of the biggest benefits (or reliefs) for creating a budget and sticking to it is that it will ensure that there will be money in your account to pay your bills—and that you will pay them on time. This in turn gives you a good credit record, also called a *credit rating*. Is that important? Yes! If you wish to fulfill your goals and dreams, it is **vital** to have a squeaky-clean, rosy-cheeked credit record.

Your credit report is a written, public record of your entire credit history and tells exactly how faithful you are—or aren't—in paying your bills. You get a bad credit record by forgetting to pay bills or failing to repay debts.

Who gets to look at your credit report? Employers thinking of hiring you, landlords wondering if they should rent to you, banks thinking of loaning you money—all of these people can obtain a copy of your credit record. The bad news is that they are specifically looking for dirty laundry.

If you pay your bills on time and never miss a payment, you will have a good credit rating. Neglect to pay overdue phone bills, shove that "Last Notice" in a drawer and forget about it, and the phone company will cut off your phone. Worse yet, that report will go on your credit record and stay there. For the next seven years, whenever you try to take out a loan, buy a car, get a mortgage, that phone bill will rear its ugly head up to shout "No!" and put your dreams on hold.

The moral of the story? If you ever want to reach your goals and dreams, you must develop a budget and start living by it.

CHAPTER 5

The Long and the Short of It

The Long and the Short of It

Short-Range Plans

Your *Life/Financial Plan* is made up of both short-term goals and long-term goals. Now that you've hammered out the first draft of a budget, you've taken care of all of your monthly expenses. You've also started to take care of short-term goals.

A *short-term goal* is something that you have to save for for a few months—or even one year—to buy. If you need a new couch, microwave oven, or some other not-so-expensive (but not-so-cheap) item, and there's not enough money in your budget to pay for it this month, you'll have to save for it. Short-range plans or goals also include saving money for emergencies or for paying taxes.

Short-range *personal* goals are often luxury or nonessential items. If you want a $100 leather jacket but your Clothing budget only allows you to spend $50 each month, you'll need to save your clothing money for two months to buy that jacket. If you want a new couch, that must come from Other in your $300/month Housing budget. Money for annual vacations must come from your Entertainment allowance. (All these short-term goals can be included on your *Life/Financial Plan* under Personal Goals.)

Long-Range Plans and Goals

Long-term expenses are goals you must save for for a couple of years—or even several decades—to reach. These include some of your personal goals (a car or house) and goals that will take you toward your life's vision (education).

The dollar amounts for some of these goals are huge, and it takes a long time to save money for them. But don't let the totals scare you. With a little patience and time, these goals are reachable. Millions of Americans buy a car, go to college, get married, and buy a house. You can too!

1. *Buying a car:* You can pick up a junker for $400, but, on the average, a good used car costs $10,000. Saving up for it could mean not paying $1–2,000 in interest.

2. *College education:* The average cost of a four-year college degree is $40,000. If you think God wants you to go to college, you'll need to do some serious saving. It would be wise, for example, to not buy a car, use public transportation, and put your Auto money toward your college education.

3. *Getting married:* Most of us eventually get married, but there's a price tag attached to the rings, rice, and reception. On the average, a wedding costs about $20,000.

4. *Buying a house:* Houses are very expensive, and you'll need to pay around $10,000 up front for a typical down payment—let alone keep up your mortgage payments later.

5. *Retirement:* You will get old one day. You may not think that it's worth saving money for retirement, but you'll have a different viewpoint when you're 68—guaranteed. But by then it will be too late. So start now.

6. *Dreams and goals:* These can be anything from a 30-foot boat to a dream vacation to taking a two-month missions trip. Most of these kind of dreams cost money.

Saving for Long-Range Goals

We have covered the topic of saving for long-range goals quite thoroughly in the book *Your First Savings Plan* in this series and recommend that you read that book to get more details. But let's cover a few points here.

You now have a budget, but where does the money you need for your long-range goals come from? That comes from your monthly budget too. The money you faithfully set aside in Savings month after month, year after year, will slowly add up until it becomes a considerable fund. Proverbs 13:11 says, "He who gathers money little by little makes it grow."

You will have noticed that, on the *Monthly Income &
Expenses* chart, we suggest you put 5 percent of your income

into Savings. This amount is really only the starting place, but we start here because many people simply cannot afford to set aside more than that in long-term savings each month.

However, when you're young with your life ahead of you, you need to start saving toward some long-term goals and need to save more than 5 percent of your NSI to reach them.

Make a Start

Take stock at this point and make a list of things you need to save for. Here we are specifically talking about the chunky, long-term savings you need to reach long-term goals and dreams. Estimate how much each goal will cost.

Photocopy the following list and write your figures in. For example, when saving for a car, write in the total amount needed under Cost. Then, under Monthly, write what you can save toward that goal each month. (You get this figure from the Auto category on your budget with maybe some of your 5 percent Savings going toward it too.) Under When, write the month and year when you'll have the full amount saved. Then transfer these numbers to your *Life/ Financial Plan* at the end of chapter 2.

Long-Term Savings	Cost	Monthly	When
1. Saving for Car	$_____	$_____	_____
2. College (education)	$_____	$_____	_____
3. Wedding	$_____	$_____	_____
4. Job Loss Funds	$_____	$_____	_____
5. Urgent Giving	$_____	$_____	_____
7. Buying a Home	$_____	$_____	_____
8. Retirement Savings	$_____	$_____	_____
9. Mission Goals	$_____	$_____	_____
10. Other	$_____	$_____	_____
11. Other	$_____	$_____	_____
Totals	$_____	$_____	_____

Establishing Checkpoints

Earlier we stated that to reach your goals and dreams you must have a time schedule and checkpoints along the way to measure actual progress against predicted progress—reality checks to verify whether you are still on schedule. By writing dates on your *Life/Financial Plan*—when you expect to have the money for each goal—you have already created a rough time frame. Since you will be pacing yourself by those dates, review them to make sure they are as realistic as possible. This way you won't be discouraged trying to meet impossible deadlines.

What checkpoints will help make sure you're going to meet your major goals? One of your best checkpoints, believe it or not, is your monthly budget. If you have determined that you're going to save $200 a month toward your college education, the best way to stay on track is to stay faithful to your monthly budget.

Your monthly budget is definitely a plan you want to keep a very close eye on, but if you have a 10-year goal, there's quite a leap between one month and 10 years. It wouldn't be smart to go 10 years without checking to see how your savings are doing. This is why we suggest that you have intermediate checkpoints.

Quarterly and Annual Checks

The chart on page 37 allows you to log your expenses and savings each quarter (every three months), as well as add them up once a year. This allows you to go in for a financial checkup every three months, take your pulse, and see what kind of shape you're in.

You may have a good monthly budget, but unexpected bills (that exceed your emergency funds) can take their toll. If you have an accident or a sickness, you may have to reduce giving toward a Savings goal to cover that emergency—either that or go in debt, which we do *not* recommend. Checking on your progress every three months is a good way to find out if you're still on track or dropping behind.

Using the *Quarterly & Annual Budget* on page 37, total all your spending and saving categories every three months. For example, if you're saving $200/month for college, then in the first quarter (Qtr. 1—January to March), write $600 in your Budget column. Beside that, in the Actual column, write how much you actually saved. Did you save $600, or only $450?

A shortfall in one quarter may not be a disaster. An emergency may simply have come up. But if you find yourself writing $500 in the *next* quarter's Actual column, $350 in the third quarter, and $400 in the fourth quarter, what you have is a pattern, not a one-time slip. And these shortfalls add up—or maybe we should say *subtract*. Instead of having $2,400 saved at the end of the year, you will only have $1,700. And if you're experiencing shortfalls in all your Actual categories, you're in trouble.

This could mean your spending habits are still out of control (see chapter 7) or that your budget was unrealistic. You'll have to decide which it is and make adjustments. You'll also have to adjust the dates in the When column of your *Life/Financial Plan* to reflect your new reality.

Make an enlarged photocopy of this chart and keep it in your accordion folder (which we explain how to set up in the next chapter). If you're faithful to fill in the Budget and Actual columns every quarter, at the end of the year you'll merely need to add up all the totals to get a yearly tally. After you fill these *Quarterly &Annual Budget* sheets out, keep them in your accordion folder also.

Five-Year and Ten-Year Plans

Quarterly and annual checkups are great, but it also helps to establish further checkpoints, and putting them at the five- and ten-year marks can be especially helpful. Look at your Mission Statement and Personal Goals and decide where you want to be five years from now and ten years from now.

Choose one or more of your intermediate goals that you can reach in five years (or less), take your *Quarterly & Annual Budget,* and in the 5-Year Goal space, write down that goal with the year that it is to be accomplished in. This will keep that goal before your eyes and mind. When you do your annual budget/ evaluation, assess your progress toward that goal.

When you achieve it, write the next intermediate goal in its place.

Quarterly & Annual Budget

Mission Statement:

_____

_____

_____

Category	Q1 Budget	Q1 Actual	Q2 Budget	Q2 Actual	Q3 Budget	Q3 Actual	Q4 Budget	Q4 Actual	Total Budget	Total Actual	**Goal**
Charitable Giving	—	—	—	—	—	—	—	—	—	—	—
Tax	—	—	—	—	—	—	—	—	—	—	—
Housing											
Down payment	—	—	—	—	—	—	—	—	—	—	—
Food	—	—	—	—	—	—	—	—	—	—	—
Auto(s)											
Total expenses	—	—	—	—	—	—	—	—	—	—	—
Saving for auto	—	—	—	—	—	—	—	—	—	—	—
Emergency fund	—	—	—	—	—	—	—	—	—	—	—
Insurance											
Life	—	—	—	—	—	—	—	—	—	—	—
Medical	—	—	—	—	—	—	—	—	—	—	—
Other	—	—	—	—	—	—	—	—	—	—	—
Debts											
Credit cards	—	—	—	—	—	—	—	—	—	—	—
Loans/Notes	—	—	—	—	—	—	—	—	—	—	—
Other	—	—	—	—	—	—	—	—	—	—	—
Ent/Recreation											
Savings goal	—	—	—	—	—	—	—	—	—	—	—
Clothing											
Savings goal	—	—	—	—	—	—	—	—	—	—	—
Savings											
College	—	—	—	—	—	—	—	—	—	—	—

	Q1 Budget	Q1 Actual	Q2 Budget	Q2 Actual	Q3 Budget	Q3 Actual	Q4 Budget	Q4 Actual	Total Budget	Total Actual	**Goal**
Marriage	—	—	—	—	—	—	—	—	—	—	—
Retirement	—	—	—	—	—	—	—	—	—	—	—
Medical Expen.											
Doctor	—	—	—	—	—	—	—	—	—	—	—
Dental	—	—	—	—	—	—	—	—	—	—	—
Other	—	—	—	—	—	—	—	—	—	—	—
Miscellaneous											
Savings goal	—	—	—	—	—	—	—	—	—	—	—
Gifts	—	—	—	—	—	—	—	—	—	—	—
Other	—	—	—	—	—	—	—	—	—	—	—
	—	—	—	—	—	—	—	—	—	—	—
5-Year Goal	—	—	—	—	—	—	—	—	—	—	—
Total Expenses	—	—	—	—	—	—	—	—	—	—	—

Returns of Joy

It takes diligence and work to track a budget every month, every quarter, and every year. On top of this, you have to pick a day four times a year to check your financial pulse. To make sure you don't get weary along the way, set some short-term personal goals that will bring you a return of joy.

You just don't want to reach your dreams at the end of your life. Make some of your goals shorter term, and make them fun or fulfilling—whether a vacation or a missions trip. God wants you to enjoy the journey.

When You Reach Goals

Every month you will allot a certain amount of dollars for each goal in the various categories. If you decide, for example, that you need $2,000 in Contingency funds to cover unexpected emergencies, and put $100/month into that fund, after twenty months, you'll have reached your goal. Then what do you do with the $100 each month? Don't keep adding it to your Contingency fund if it has enough. Reallocate the money to another needy fund.

CHAPTER 6

Getting Organized

"I used to throw *everything* into a big ol' shoebox. This works much better."

Getting Organized

The Need to Be Organized

If you had to find all your bills right now, where would you look? On top of your fridge? Under your couch cushions? In your sock drawer? In the garbage? If you grinned sheepishly at any of these questions . . . *hoo boy!* Read on.

"God is not a God of disorder but of peace" (1 Corinthians 14:33), so it would seem that He wants *you* to be organized as well. True or false? True. First Corinthians 14:40 says, "Everything should be done in a fitting and orderly way." Do these verses describe the way you've organized your financial papers? If not, then look out! It's. . . .

Time to Get Organized

If all you can do today before sundown is to designate a shoe box or some other box as your financial file, do that. Stop reading after this paragraph, grab a box, go through your house, dig out any and all financial records, and drop them into the box. (This includes warranties, bank statements, returned checks, bills, income statements, and warning letters from the IRS.)

Ideally, you need an accordion file where you can keep— and organize—your financial records. Many such files come already labeled with financial categories. So at your next opportunity go out and buy one. Then *use* it. Every time a bill comes in the mail, file it. Then when your paycheck comes you can go straight to your bills, pull them out, and pay them.

Crown Financial Ministries also has excellent financial organizers. Get online, go to *www.cfcministry.org,* and click on *Resources* in the right-hand column. The Bill Organizer is a transparent plastic expanding file with 12 tabbed pockets to help you organize your bills; the Cash Organizer—perfect for students—will help you track your spending and keep a running balance for each budget category.

Sample Filing System

Here are examples of the kinds of categories you should file financial papers under:

1. *Warranties:* These are very valuable papers. Being able to find a warranty could save you hundreds of dollars.

2. *Bank statements:* You need to check these against the numbers recorded in your home ledger. Or, if you have a passbook, be sure your passbook is faithfully updated.

3. *Bills:* Fail to pay a bill on time and it could be a black mark on your credit record. File all your bills together or by category (phone, cable, etc.), whichever works best for you.

4. *Returned checks:* These prove that you paid your bills. File them according to their various categories.

5. *Insurance:* These documents are even more valuable than warranties. These papers are worth big, *big* bucks!

6. *Financing documents:* If you have legal papers regarding a loan, you simply do *not* want to lose them.

7. *Investments:* Here keep records of stocks, mutual funds, or other investments.

8. *Taxes:* This is the place for papers related to taxes—receipts for charitable giving and income statements.

When to Pay Bills

Bills come due at different times and people pay their bills in different ways. You might pay all of your bills by check. You might pay them at the ATM machine, through a bank teller, over the phone, or even over the Internet. You need to find a bill-paying system that works for you and stick to it.

If you get paid once a month, it's a matter of watching over the money in your checking account to make sure it lasts long enough to cover a month's worth of bills. If you get paid twice monthly—once on the 15th and again at the end of the month—take time out twice a month to pay your bills.

File your bills in a "To Pay" file in your folder and pay close attention to the "Due" date on each bill, and be very sure that you pay that bill before that date passes.

Recording Your Transactions

There is not enough space in this chapter to give you a detailed explanation on how to fill out a checkbook ledger or reconcile a checking account. These subjects have been covered in great detail in other books from Crown Financial Ministries, such as *The Financial Planning Workbook* and *Money Matters for Teens Workbook*. These are excellent resources and are well worth owning.

There are some excellent reasons for keeping accurate track of your financial transactions. One of them is so that if the bank makes a mistake—and they sometimes do—you will catch it. Also, knowing exactly how much money you have left in your account allows you to go to sleep in peace at night knowing that none of your checks are about to bounce. Plus, you'll know that you're on your way to your dreams.

The traditional way to track your finances is to log all income and expenses in a home ledger. These days, of course, you can do the same thing on computer, using . . .

Financial Software

There are a number of software programs available to help you organize your finances. However, when it comes to software that does all that—and is based upon godly, biblical principles—you simply can't beat the ones developed by Crown Financial Ministries (CFM). These can also be found on its Web site *www.cfcministry.org* under *Resources*.

For young adults, perhaps the most helpful software is CFM's *Money Matters Basic*. It will allow you to keep track of your bills and pay them on time; help you track your checking, savings, loans, credit/debit cards, and income; give you biblically based advice; and show you the benefits of paying off debts early by using the debt elimination plan.

Whatever system you have for keeping and organizing your financial records, be sure to use it.

CHAPTER 7

Reining in Wild Horses

Reining in Wild Horses

Required: Self-Control

What have we learned so far? First, that in order to reach your dreams and goals you must have a written plan of where you're going, you must know how much each goal in that plan costs, and you must know how long it will take to save to reach that goal. Second, you have also seen that your monthly budget, with your annual budget, is the cornerstone of a successful financial plan. Good for you! And you now actually have a monthly budget and an annual budget, rough-hewn as they may be.

But a budget will do you no good unless you actually use it. While this would seem like a no-brainer, people often write out financial plans that they never put into action. They continue overspending, sliding down the slippery slope of debt, ever further away from their goals—all for lack of using a budget. Why, if something could literally make your dreams come true, would it fall to the wayside like a New Year's resolution to stay off chocolate?

There are several reasons: Implementing a budget is—in the beginning—hard work; it requires discipline; it requires you to rein in any wild spending habits; it requires you to live within your means and not spend more than you earn; it requires you to stop impulse buying. In short, you must exercise self-control. But hey! Good news! Self-control is a virtue! Galatians 5:23 calls it a fruit of the Spirit.

Overspending will get you into debt. If you are struggling under a load of debt, you know just how true this is. A budget is the way out of bondage, the surest way to fulfill your dreams. In fact, unless a gold meteorite craters in your backyard, it is just about the only way.

Spending and Self-Esteem

OK, so you need to exercise some self-control and rein in your spending habits, but how? The answer depends on why you're overspending. Here is where we need to deal with core issues and ask some hard questions. If you've been overspending simply because you had no idea that budgets existed, exercising self-control may not be difficult. Now that you have a budget to help you realize your dreams, you're probably eager to implement it. But what if the problem goes deeper?

Sociologists tell us that people often spend their money to gain power, freedom, and security—and to buy things that enhance their sense of self-esteem and project the "right" image so that they'll be accepted and loved. If you're spending to impress others, brace yourself: You need to ponder the core issues of Christianity.

The apostle John said, "Everything in the world—the cravings of sinful man, the lust of his eyes and the boasting of what he has and does—comes not from the Father but from the world. The world and its desires pass away, but the man who does the will of God lives forever" (1 John 2:16–17).

God knows your core needs, and He is there at the deepest levels to meet those needs. This is why understanding stewardship is so liberating. When you realize that God is the ultimate source of all blessing and security—financial, emotional, or otherwise—it frees you from worry. After all, the Bible promises that "God will meet *all* your needs" (Philippians 4:19, emphasis added).

But if you try to meet your deepest needs through things rather than God, whatever security and acceptance you buy will be temporary. How can material things bring lasting joy? Jesus said, "A man's life does not consist in the abundance of his possessions" (Luke 12:15). We all want to be accepted, but an inordinate need for social acceptance can wreak havoc with your spending habits and make you unnecessarily generous to those you want to accept you.

Dealing with Instant Gratification

Too many people have a need for instant gratification. When something desirable catches their eye, they make a snap decision that they must have it. And they want it *now*. The thought barely occurs to them that they don't have the money to buy it. After all, they live in a "buy now, pay later" world.

No money? No problem! They pull out the magic lamp of their credit card and a powerful genie with a $2,500 credit line instantly appears to grant them as many wishes as they want. No joke! Recently a brochure was mailed out, entitled *2001 Wish List*. Beside a picture of a genie smoking out of a lamp was an appeal to take out a loan to make dreams come true. It asked: "Why put off until tomorrow what you can do today?" (There was a good reason for putting *this* company off: They charged 24 percent interest.)

This "buy now, pay later" mentality is expensive because credit cards charge high interest rates. Fewer than 40 percent of Americans who own credit cards pay the full balance owed each month, which means that 60 percent of Americans with wish lists and credit cards are in debt! As Proverbs 21:17 says, "He who loves pleasure will become poor."

You need to take an ax to this kind of thinking with the same intensity with which Jack took out the beanstalk. Giving in to instant gratification usually means giving in to "the lust of [your] eyes." Buying for the wrong motives will blow your budget. Even if you see something that you genuinely need, you should only buy it if and when you have the cash to do so.

You Deserve It! You're Worth It!

Here's a motivator that's used blatantly in advertising today: As you sit vegging out in front of your TV after a hard day's work, exhausted and susceptible, commercials come on, saying, "Buy this expensive toy! Can't afford it? Buy it anyway. You deserve it!" Moments later another ad says, "Go on a dream vacation! Can't pay for it? Take out a loan. You're worth it!"

Oh? And what about most of the rest of the world who can't afford these things and aren't eligible for credit cards to get them with? Aren't they worthy too? When you put things in this perspective, it's easy to see that you need to aim a clicker at these materialistic commercials: Not only do they advocate unbiblical practices, but they stand in stark contrast to the reality that billions face. Much of the earth's population has no choice but to agree with the apostle Paul when he said, "But if we have food and clothing, we will be content with that" (1 Timothy 6:8).

This should apply to all of us. As long as we live on Planet Earth, the Bible advises, "Keep your lives free from the love of money and be content with what you have" (Hebrews 13:5).

Living Within Your Means

The ads tell you you're worth a million dollars. Your bank book tells you you're worth $837.67. Which are you going to believe? It's important that you aren't foggy on this issue, because what you believe determines how you will handle your money and how you will view credit card spending and installment plan purchases.

If you have bought into modern advertising, you will ignore your pitiful little bank statement. You'll pull out your credit card and enjoy the life you feel you deserve to live. However, if you want to avoid a life of debt, ignore the ads and enjoy the life you can afford to pay for.

Smelling the Coffee

The best way to determine whether you are living within your budget or not is to subtract your monthly expenses from your monthly income and see whether you have a surplus or a deficit. On a separate sheet of blank paper make a couple of charts like the one below. On the first chart, fill in the totals for the last three months. Use the second copy to track your income for this month and the next two months.

If you have money left over at the end of a month, you have a surplus. If you spent more than you earned, you have a deficit. If you really want to smell the coffee and see where your finances are at, this little chart is an expresso without sugar or cream.

Months (*names*)			
Total Income	$_____	$_____	$_____
Total Expenses	$_____	$_____	$_____
Surplus or Deficit	$_____	$_____	$_____

If you have more expenses than income, find out where you've overspent and repent. Check your budget and see where you can make cuts and decide which purchases to put off for now. However, if you have more income than expenses, put the extra into Savings—you're already on your way to your dreams. Channel that extra cash down the right pipes and you're off!

CHAPTER 8

Dealing with Debt

"I just about figured it out. It looks like we go further into debt every month from buying 'calculator paper'"

Dealing with Debt

Are You in Debt?

You may have a vague idea that you owe money to people, but you need to seriously ask yourself, "Am I in debt? If so, how deeply?" You already have the numbers from chapter 3, "A Polaroid of Your Pocketbook," where you wrote out your liabilities (debts). You also have the surplus/deficit from chapter 7. Refer back to those numbers now. Then check Yes or No beside each statement below. Too many Yeses and you're in debt—and you need to make some changes quickly!

Debt Problems Assessment Sheet

Yes	No	
____	____	I often pay bills late.
____	____	I sometimes pay only part of my phone bill (or miss paying it entirely) so I can pay other bills.
____	____	I have no money saved in a Contingency fund. If an emergency hits, I'm forced to use my credit card.
____	____	My credit cards are just about maxed out.
____	____	I'm not really sure how much interest I'm paying on my credit cards or store cards.
____	____	I make the minimum payment on my credit card bill.
____	____	I often use a credit card to pay for things like food.
____	____	I don't like to think about debt. It just depresses me.
____	____	I'm not exactly sure how much money I owe.
____	____	I receive calls and unpleasant letters from creditors.
____	____	I'm filling this out while sitting in Debtor's Prison.

Foxes and Compound Interest

Song of Songs 2:15 talks about "the little foxes that ruin the vineyards." Yes, it is the little things that can bring your finances to ruin. Let's consider one of the most nefarious little foxes that can ravage your financial vineyard—compound interest.

When the fine print on your credit card statement says your interest is "calculated daily," you are paying not only interest on the amount you owe (simple interest) but interest on the interest itself—compound interest.

Let's say that you have a credit card where you pay 12 percent on overdue charges. This 12 percent is your annual percentage rate (APR), the cost of credit on a yearly basis. This yearly sum calculated as a daily sum, which in this case comes out to about a third of a cent on every dollar per day. That may not sound like much, and it adds up slowly at first, but let those little foxes have the run of the vineyard for a few months and they'll end up fat and sleek-furred, but your grapes will be gone.

The Rule of 72

If you are saving money in a bank, the *Rule of 72* will work for you to increase your riches. If you owe money and are slow at paying it back, this rule is working against you every day.

The Rule of 72 determines how many years it will take for your investment or your debt to double. Divide 72 by the percentage rate you are paying on your debt or earning on your savings. Let's say you have a savings account with $1,000 in it. It earns 4 percent interest from the bank. Seventy-two divided by four is eighteen. If you make no further deposits, it will take eighteen years for your $1,000 to double to $2,000.

Now let's say you racked up $1,000 on a credit card charges a mere 12 percent interest. Seventy-two divided by twelve is six. If you didn't make any payments, it would take only six years for your debt to double to $2,000.

Of course, both your debts and your savings can double more than once. Let's say you decide to leave your investment in the bank for thirty-six years without cashing it in. (Divide the years you will leave it in by the number of years it takes to double each time.) Your original $1,000 has now become $4,000. The higher rate of interest you are paid, the faster your money doubles.

Now think about how much faster your credit card debts can double. If you're paying 12 percent interest or—perish the thought!—even more, you can see that it is urgent that you pay off that debt as soon as possible. (For more details, see chapter 5 of *Getting Your First Credit Card,* another book in this series.)

Getting Out of Debt

But what if you're already in debt? What if you have a student loan, have maxed out your credit card, and are swamped with monthly bills? Is it too late? Are you doomed? Fortunately, the answer is no. You can get out of debt and get back on track if you take the following steps right now:

- *Cutting up:* Get a pair of scissors and cut up any credit card with an outstanding balance. If you cannot pay the amount owed this month—right now—cut your card up.

- *Cutting back:* The second step is to immediately cut back on spending. Change your spending habits. It's bad enough to be in debt, but you can at least stop getting deeper into it.

- *Cutting edge:* A budget is your cutting edge weapon against debt. Write in all expenses and decide what percentage of your budget you'll use to pay debts.

- *Cutting slack:* Cut yourself some slack by having a realistic repayment schedule. If you allot too much of your budget to paying debts, you'll live too austerely, get frustrated, and give up. Pace yourself. You're in this for the long haul.

- *Cutting out:* Cut out surprises. If you have no Contingency funds set aside, start a fund today. Have money to meet surprise bills and you won't have to go in debt to pay them.

- *Cutting salami:* You might want to take on a second job— say, cutting salami—to pay your debts down more quickly.

Do yourself a favor: Get out of debt and save for your future. Set yourself on the track to your dreams.

CHAPTER 9

Increasing Your Earnings

"I *thought* it was you. Found that second job, huh?"

Mama Gina's PIZZA

2 for 1 SALE
All medium Pizzas

Increasing Your Earnings

Improving Your Earning Potential

Generally, the solution to "not enough money" is not to earn more money but to learn to budget and not spend more than you earn. But if you're already doing these things and it's still going to take you years to pay off your debts at your present rate, it may be worthwhile to push a little harder to get debt-free sooner. The sooner your debts are out of the way, the sooner you have a clear shot at your goals.

Even if you're not in debt, you might have come to some sobering conclusions after crunching the numbers for your long-range goals. It might be obvious that, at your present rate, you'll be ready to collect old age pension by the time you have money saved up for college. If this is the case, it's wise to consider shifting gears, moving into the fast lane, and pressing the pedal to the metal for a while.

Take a long look at your financial plan. That will help you decide if you need to get serious about earning more money. Have you figured out how long it will take you to reach your goals? Are you concerned that they're taking too long? Don't want to live too Spartan a life while saving for long-term dreams? Want to do something about it? You have several options.

Second Jobs and Savings

One of the most common things people do when they need to earn or save more money is to take on a second job. If you can convince yourself (and your friends) that you need to sacrifice a chunk of your social life for a few months or a couple of years in order to put your debts behind you—or save money for your long-range goals—go for it. (This is more realistic when you're single and don't have a spouse to consider.)

You can earn money slowly but surely, even if you have a near-minimum wage job and take on a second job also at minimum wage. You can save money, but the key word here is *slowly*. On the other hand, *surely* also applies. (See Proverbs 13:11.)

If you faithfully squirrel away modest amounts of money in savings accounts or mutual funds that pay compound interest, your cash will work for you to earn money. Hey! If *you* have to work extra hard, why should you let your *savings* lie around doing nothing? Put your savings to work too!

Get a Raise

So you've got a good job . . . but you've still got a ways to go to achieve your life mission. Instead of reconciling yourself to plodding along at the same rate for years, look for ways to increase your earning potential and thus your income.

The first way is to be the kind of worker who deserves a raise. Give your all to your job and obey Ecclesiastes 9:10, which says, "Whatever your hand finds to do, do it with all your might." As a result you should expect to be rewarded for outstanding service. Hard workers are often noticed and earmarked for a raise.

Unfortunately, sometimes the extra effort you put into your job might be overlooked. If you think that you're a valuable asset to your company—you've always done your best, have done more than was expected, have stepped in during emergencies—and it slips your boss's mind to give you that raise, you might want to bring the subject up. This is especially true if it's *time* for a raise, or if other workers are paid more but do less. Bosses recognize superior workers and hate to lose them, so ask politely for a raise. Just make sure you deserve one.

The "*Give That Person a Raise!*" Checklist

___ Good attitude	___ Hard worker	___ Cheerful
___ Responsible	___ Good people skills	___ Prompt
___ Conscientious	___ Willing to learn	___ Diligent
___ Takes courses	___ Asks questions	___ Motivated
___ Meets deadlines	___ Willing to go the extra mile	

Make Yourself More Valuable

This is a second way to increase your income. One of the things on the checklist was "Takes courses." Taking courses and attending work-related seminars is an excellent way to make yourself more valuable at your job. Quite a number of courses will help you move up at work: courses in stress management, interpersonal relationships, computer upgrading, first aid, etc. Also consider volunteering for special projects at work that will give you experience in new areas or provide a showcase for your talents. Sometimes even doing volunteer work in your community will increase your experience and knowledge in key areas.

Often you can make yourself more valuable with only a modest investment of your time and money. That modest investment could pay off big time the day the boss gives you a raise or when he or she has to lay off a worker. If there's no difference between you and the next person except that you know first aid and have extra computer skills, guess who's more valuable to the company and who stays? You!

Find a Higher-Paying Job

A third way to boost your income might be to move on. If you've made yourself valuable to the company, need a raise, and have asked for one (but the boss said no), it may be time to look for another job. You are not obliged to stay at that job if there's another job that meshes better with your life goals and pays more. It may simply be that there are no opportunities at your company for further advancement. If the company is too small, or someone only moves up the chain of command when an overseer dies, you might need to move on.

If you are considering taking a better-paying job, however, remember that jobs that pay better also require extra education and skills that you may not have.

To School and Back

That brings us to the fourth way to increase your earning potential: increasing your knowledge and/or skills. Getting the needed education or skills often means taking extra courses or going to a university or a trade school.

If you put out $10,000 to upgrade your education and it can lead to a promotion or a new job that pays $4,000 more a year, you earn your investment back in two years and six months. After that it's profit. Not bad! But not all upgrading costs big bucks. A $400 seminar could lead to a raise. (If you are thinking of going to a university or college, we recommend that you read the other book in this series, *Preparing for College*.) Life doesn't remain static! As you keep growing, improving your skills, and working diligently, things can dramatically improve. You can increase your income so that you can come closer to your goals sooner.

Even if you have to go to night school or take intense week-end courses, consider that time and energy commitment as the bottom booster rocket that does most of the initial hard work getting the load off the ground, fighting inertia and gravity, slowly but surely rising up until—bingo!—you've gained key knowledge or skills and the first spent booster drops away. When your hard work results in a raise, a promotion, or a better job, the second booster engine cuts in. Now you're higher and have some real momentum! That second booster screaming through the upper atmosphere will help to lift the final payload high into orbit where your goals are—but it couldn't get there without the first booster.

No matter which method (or methods) you choose to use to increase your earning potential, and therefore your income, remember the reason you're doing it. It's not just to live a more luxurious lifestyle or up your spending. Your new NSI amount goes into your budget and is allocated so that you move another step toward your goals and to what God designed you to do.

CHAPTER 10

Implementing Your Plan

Implementing Your Plan

The Time Has Come

If you've prayed and received counsel, and both God and godly people feel the *Life/Financial Plan* you've developed is sane and attainable, what do you do? *Implement* it, of course! Keep it with your monthly and annual budgets and other financial papers in your accordion folder where you won't lose it. Refer to it often and stick to it! When your paycheck comes in, pay your bills, then faithfully stash away money toward each of your savings goals.

Whether you use a home ledger or financial software, keep an up-to-date, accurate record of your income, deposits, and expenses. Be sure to file away all financial records in an orderly fashion, on the day you receive them. Log all expenses the day you incur them. Also, record deposits or withdrawals done at ATM machines and purchases made with your bank card the day you make them. This way, you won't forget.

Monitor Your Progress

Back in chapter 5 we showed you how to set up checkpoints to measure actual progress against predicted progress. You must use these checkpoints—particularly forms like the *Quarterly & Annual Budget*—to make sure you stay on track and on schedule.

Having a written record of your progress not only keeps things accurate, it can greatly encourage you to save. Each month you can watch your savings grow. For a more visual encouragement, you might even want to draw a bar graph, with each of your savings goals as different-colored bars, and add to them every month as your savings increase.

Remember, don't get so caught up with your month to month budget that you forget where you're heading. You should regularly (at least annually) look at your Mission Statement and see how much closer you are to achieving it. Make sure you haven't gotten sidetracked on to some other goal.

If there is someone whom you trust and can talk to freely, make yourself accountable to that person. This doesn't have to be the president of a bank—although that would be great—but merely a good friend who feels free to tell you the truth. Meet with him or her every week or month to talk over what you've accomplished and the areas you're struggling with. "Two are better than one . . . if one falls down, his friend can help him up" (Ecclesiastes 4:9–10). Perhaps he or she would like to make a *Life/Financial Plan* and work toward life goals as well.

Modify As Needed

You should stick to your written budget. On the other hand, you must allow flexibility in your planning. If you get a raise or change jobs, change your budget—but keep most expenses the same and put the difference toward goals. Also, remember, God has the really long-range vision and can see the entire game board from His vantage point. In your own interests, He may redirect your career path or fine-tune it. That would change your financial plan. You need to be open to such changes.

Also, when first setting up a budget, it may be necessary to borrow from one account to supplement another. For example, if your car breaks down before you've accumulated enough savings in your Auto account, it may be necessary to borrow from the Clothing or Entertainment categories to pay for the repair. However, you should not do this month after month. That would defeat the purpose of budgeting. And remember to repay those accounts out of your Auto category next month.

Finally . . . once you have developed a plan, stick to it. Keep your goal in mind and pace yourself to ensure that you'll be able to go the distance. Remember the story of the tortoise and the hare. You may feel like a tortoise at times as you move one step at a time toward your distant goals, but given time, your goals will no longer be distant. You will be there!

Glossary

Budget: A specific, written plan where you allot a percentage of your income to each category of bills and expenses.

Checkpoints: A series of short-range goals used to measure actual progress against predicted progress. These reality checks verify whether you are on track and on schedule.

Credit rating: A record of your entire credit history, good and bad. Banks, employers, or landlords can check up on you by accessing your credit records.

Dreams: A personal goal, something you want to accomplish with your life. It's often unrelated to your work.

Financial plan: A written plan that shows how much each of your dreams and goals will cost and how soon the money can be saved to make them become real.

Goals: These are part of your life's mission. These are specific things you set out to do, focus on, and save money for. Examples are going to college, coaching Little League, buying a house, etc.

Life plan: A written list of what you believe God wants you to do with your life, usually based upon your talents and desires. It includes your short-term and long-term goals, both career and personal.

Mission statement: A brief summary of where you want to be at the end of your life, the goal you aim your time, energy, and money toward. What God designed you for.

Net Spendable Income: After you've given to God and paid your taxes, this is the money left over from your paycheck, with which you pay your monthly bills and accomplish your dreams.

Net worth: Where you stand financially at a given moment in time. Your total money and possessions (assets) minus your total debts (liabilities).

Stewardship: Managing God's resources. God owns everything, including what we consider "our" possessions; He has made us the stewards (managers) of His property.

Index

auto, buying 33
bills 41–42
budget 26–30, 44, 61
  Quarterly & Annual 36–38
charitable giving 28
checkpoints 10, 35–36, 60–61
compound interest 51
contentment 45–47
credit card 46, 51
credit rating/record 12, 30
debt 44, 50–52
deficit 36, 47
desires 14
discipleship 15–16
dreams 14, 33
education 10, 33, 56–57
emergencies 12, 35, 38, 52
expenses 29–30
  tracking 24, 42, 47
filing system 40–41
financial personality 20–21
financial plan
  benefits of 9–12
  lack of 8–9, 10–11
goals
  intermediate 9
  long-term 32–34
  prioritzing 12
  short-term 32
house, buying 33

impulse buying 12, 44
income, increasing 54–57
instant gratification 45–46
Life/Financial Plan 9, 16–17, 18
marriage 33
mission statement 16
Net Spendable Income (NSI) 29
net worth 23
organized, getting 22, 34,
  40–42, 60
personality test 15
prayer 14–15
raise, getting a 55–56
retirement 33
Rule of 72 51–52
second job 52, 54–55
security 45
self-control 44–48, 52
self-esteem 44–45
taxes 29
vision 16
worry 11, 12

building Christian faith in families

Lightwave Publishing is one of North America's leading developers of quality resources that encourage, assist, and equip parents to build Christian faith in their families. Lightwave's products help parents answer their children's questions about the Christian faith, teach them how to make church, Sunday school, and Bible reading more meaningful for their children, provide them with pointers on teaching their children to pray, and much, much more.

Lightwave, together with its various publishing and ministry partners, such as Focus on the Family, has been successfully producing innovative books, music, and games since 1984. Some of its more recent products include the *Parents' Guide to the Spiritual Growth of Children*, *My Time With God*, and *Mealtime Moments*.

Lightwave also has a fun kids' Web site and an Internet-based newsletter called *Tips and Tools for Spiritual Parenting*. For more information and a complete list of Lightwave products, please visit: **www.lightwavepublishing.com**.

A MINISTRY OF MOODY BIBLE INSTITUTE

Moody Press, a ministry of Moody Bible Institute, is designed for education, evangelization, and edification.

If we may assist you in knowing more about Christ and the Christian life, please write us without obligation:

Moody Press, c/o MLM, Chicago, Illinois 60610

Or visit us at Moody's Web site: **www.moodypress.org**